CUTE AND UNUSUAL PETS

MINIATURE HORSES

by Paula Wilson

Consultant
Sarrah Kaye
Veterinarian and General Curator
Staten Island Zoo
Staten Island, New York

CAPSTONE PRESS
a capstone imprint

Snap Books are published by Capstone Press,
1710 Roe Crest Drive, North Mankato, Minnesota 56003
www.mycapstone.com

Library of Congress Cataloging-in-Publication Data
Names: Wilson, Paula M., 1963- author.
Title: Miniature horses / by Paula M. Wilson.
Description: North Mankato, Minnesota : an imprint of Capstone Press, [2019]
  | Series: Snap books. Cute and unusual pets. | Audience: Age 8-14.
Identifiers: LCCN 2018016129 (print) | LCCN 2018017759 (ebook) |
  ISBN 9781543530681 (eBook PDF) |
  ISBN 9781543530599 (hardcover)
Subjects: LCSH: Miniature horses—Juvenile literature.
Classification: LCC SF293.M56 (ebook) | LCC SF293.M56 W55 2019 (print) | DDC
  636.1/09—dc23
LC record available at https://lccn.loc.gov/2018016129

Editorial Credits
Lauren Dupuis-Perez, editor
Sara Radka, designer
Kathy McColley, production specialist

Image Credits
Getty Images: GlobalP, 1, Loshadenok, 25, Sue Barr, 17, Zuzule, 11; Newscom: Blend Images LLC, 18, MCT/Detroit Free Press/Mandi Wright, 27, NCJ Mirrorpix, 9, WENN, 28, ZUMA Press/Albuquerque Journal/Adolphe Pierre-Louis, 10, ZUMA Press/Sacramento Bee/Lezlie Sterling, 12, ZUMA Press/TASS/Demianchuk Alexander, 15; Shutterstock: Achira Muenkaew, back cover, 7, Grezova Olga, 5, Jaromir Chalabala, 6, Kachalkina Veronika, 21, MsDianaZ, 29, Vera Zinkova, 22, Zuzule, cover

Glossary terms are bolded on first use in text.

Printed and bound in the United States of America.
PA021

TABLE OF CONTENTS

CHAPTER 1
MEET THE
MINIATURE HORSE

What's the first thing you notice about miniature horses? Maybe it's how cute they are! These charming animals look just like full-sized horses, only much smaller. Miniature horses are not only adorable. They are also smart, gentle, and **affectionate.** They are social animals that like being around people. Their friendly nature and small size make them wonderful pets.

A miniature horse can be a great pet for people who might not be ready for a larger horse. Miniature horses can be easier to handle than larger horses. They need less food and do not require as much space. Owning a miniature horse has other rewards. It forms a strong bond with its owner. It becomes a part of the family.

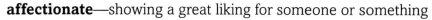

affectionate—showing a great liking for someone or something

Mini horses are herd animals and often are happiest with other horses.

SOCIAL HORSES

Miniature horses are popular on social media. Dozens of Facebook groups feature miniature horses for sale. They also show photos of everyday life with this pet. Crunch and Lippy, two miniature horses from Australia, have 232,000 followers on Instagram.

Palomino horses have a golden shade to their coats.

SMALL YET STUNNING

How big is miniature? Miniature horses weigh 150 to 250 pounds (68 to 113 kilograms). To be considered miniature, they cannot be taller than 34 inches (86 centimeters). Their height is measured from the ground to the top of their shoulders where the mane ends. What they lack in size they make up for in beauty. Miniature horses can be a variety of colors. They may be black, brown, chestnut, or gray. Some are more unusual colors called palomino and pinto. Many have speckles or spots.

SUPER SENSES

Horses' eyes are set wide apart. This lets them see a wide area at one time. Horses can see almost all the way behind themselves. They also can see very well at night. Horses have very good hearing too. This helps them sense danger. Miniature horses communicate with sounds and body language. They make snorts, **whinnies**, and squeals. A horse's ear and eye movements communicate different things, such as danger or fear.

DID YOU KNOW?

Horses, including miniature horses, cannot vomit. Food can only travel in one direction through their **digestive system.**

---

whinny—a gentle, high-pitched sound; the word is often used to describe horse sounds

digestive system—the body organs that break down food into energy and get rid of waste

HORSES FROM LONG AGO

Miniature horses are **descendants** of wild horses found throughout most of the world. Some of these horse **ancestors** are now extinct, including one called a dawn horse. Thousands of years ago, people began to **domesticate** wild horses. They used the animals for food, transportation, and farming.

People first bred miniature horses in the 1700s. European royalty got them as pets for their children. Miniature horses also worked in mines pulling heavy carts full of coal. This strong animal can pull three to four times its body weight. It could also fit into small spaces in the mines. These work horses, often known as pit ponies, worked long hours underground.

A HORSE IS A HORSE, OF COURSE

Miniature horses are different from ponies. In fact, miniature horses have more in common with full-sized horses than with ponies. Ponies have wider and shorter necks and shorter legs than horses. Their coats and manes are thicker than those of horses.

8

In the late 1800s, more than 200,000 miniature horses and ponies worked in coal mines.

Miniature horses first came to the United States in 1888. Here they also worked in coal mines. However, in the 1950s new machines could remove coal from the mines. Miniature horses were no longer needed. During this same time, miniature horses were becoming more popular as pets.

descendant—a person or animal who comes from a particular group of people or animals from the past

ancestor—a distant relative from long ago

domesticate—to tame something so that it can live with or be used by humans

CHAPTER 2
MINIATURE HORSES AS PETS

Miniature horses are popular pets in the United States and Canada. Families in England, Holland, Japan, and Australia also keep them as pets. People of all ages can enjoy having a miniature horse. Miniature horses make especially great pets for children. Kids can learn how to care for and ride a miniature horse before they move on to a full-sized horse.

SHOWING OFF

More than 250 shows for miniature horses take place each year in the United States and Canada. One is the American Miniature Horse Association World Championship in Fort Worth, Texas. Owners show off their horse's skills in dozens of categories. These include carriage driving, obstacle courses, showmanship, and jumping.

To get ready for horse shows, some owners give their miniature horses a hair cut, called clipping.

Some people keep miniature horses simply as companion pets. They spend time caring for and developing a bond with the animal. Other owners also train miniature horses to compete in shows. Owners or trainers prepare the horses for competition in different categories. One category is fence jumping. In this contest, a horse's owner runs alongside it as it leaps over obstacles.

Miniature horses are very social and need a lot of attention.

HOLD YOUR HORSES

Caring for a pet is a big responsibility. Taking care of a miniature horse requires a lot of time and commitment. The animal needs daily attention and care. Talk to your parents about owning a miniature horse. Answer these questions before you decide if a miniature horse is right for you and your family:

• How much does a miniature horse cost? Who will pay for the horse and its expenses? You or your parents?

• Do you have space in your yard for a miniature horse and a shelter for it? If not, will you be able to pay to rent space at a stable?

- If your miniature horse will live with you, do you and your family have the time to care for it, including feeding, cleaning, and hoof care? Who will take care of the miniature horse every day? Who will clean the stable? You or your parents or siblings? How will you all share in the responsibility?

- Do the vets in your area take care of miniature horses?

- Do you plan to take the miniature horse to shows and competitions? Will you need to hire a trainer to work with the animal?

- Do you need to buy a horse trailer to transport the animal? How much does a horse trailer cost? Do you have a place to store it?

WEIGHT LIMIT

If you want a pet horse that you can ride, a miniature horse may not be for you. Only people who weigh less than 70 pounds (32 kg) should ride a miniature horse. Otherwise the horse could be injured. If someone who is the right size will ride your miniature horse, make sure you have a special small saddle.

CHOOSING YOUR PET

So you've decided that a miniature horse is the right pet for you. Where do you get one? How do you decide which one to get? One option is to buy a miniature horse from a **breeder**. A breeder will help you choose your pet. He or she will also show you how to take care of it. To find a breeder in your area, visit the American Miniature Horse Association website. Another option is to contact a horse rescue or adoption agency in your area.

When choosing a miniature horse, look for one that is in good health. It should have bright eyes, a shiny coat, and well-trimmed hooves. Be sure the animal is alert and friendly. A miniature horse baby should not be taken from its mother until it is 4 to 6 months old. Your miniature horse will be fully grown by age 5. Some people buy two miniature horses so they can keep each other company. If you get both a male and a female, make sure the male has been **gelded**.

---

breeder—a person who raises animals to sell
geld—to operate on a male animal so it is unable to produce young

A miniature horse breeder is a good source of information for horse owners.

What happens if you bought a miniature horse but then realize it is not the right pet for you? Find a home for it with a breeder or with someone who wants to adopt it.

HORSE EXPERTS

The American Miniature Horse Association was established in 1978 to register miniature horses. The association is a helpful resource for miniature horse breeders and horse shows.

CHAPTER 3

CARING FOR YOUR MINIATURE HORSE

Before you bring home your new horse, make sure you have everything ready. Start with its living area. All horses, including miniature horses, need outdoor space to **graze**, run, and play. You will need a quarter to a half **acre** of land per horse. Miniature horses also need an enclosed space to shelter them from rain, wind, and other bad weather. A barn or stable is best. A three-sided structure with dirt or clay flooring and lots of air flow will also work. Your yard should be fenced in so that your horse does not run away.

DID YOU KNOW?

Horses shed their hair twice a year, once in the spring and again in the fall.

---

graze—to eat grass that is growing in a field
acre—a measurement of area equal to 43,560 square feet (4,047 square meters); an acre is about the size of a football field

Miniature horses are fun pets but are a lot of work.

STABLE FOR RENT

If you do not have room or a proper shelter for the horse in your yard, you will need to rent space in a stable. Different arrangements can be made with stables owners. Some will take care of all your horse's needs, including feeding, brushing, and cleaning. Others will house your horse, but leave the daily care of the animal to you. Be sure to find a stable specifically for miniature horses. Miniature horses can escape under stable doors made for large horses. The stable should have space for the miniature horse to sleep and a place for its feed and water.

BASIC HORSE CARE

Your miniature horse needs certain foods to keep it healthy. The animal should eat a combination of hay and grass. It also needs a salt block to provide important minerals. Small amounts of grain are okay too. Flaxseed helps give this animal a shiny coat. Also make sure your miniature horse always has fresh, clean water.

Miniature horses need daily brushing. Use a brush or comb made especially for horses. Do not bathe your horse too often. The natural oils in its coat get washed off when it is bathed.

Feed your miniature horse the right foods and make sure it gets a lot of exercise to help keep it healthy.

A horse's hooves need to be well-balanced so that it can walk properly. Use a hoof pick each day to clean out rocks from its hooves. A **farrier** trims hooves and puts horseshoes on full-sized horses. Miniature horses do not wear horseshoes, but they still need regular care from a farrier.

HORSE HEALTH

Take your miniature horse to the vet every year. The vet will provide **vaccinations** and deworming medicine if needed. He or she will also check your horse for health issues, such as **obesity** and dental problems. You can help prevent your horse from becoming obese. Do not overfeed it or give it too much grass or grain. Dental problems are common for miniature horses. Their teeth are large compared to their jaws. Dental problems can make it difficult for them to eat.

DID YOU KNOW?

Quidding is when a horse drops partially chewed food out of its mouth. This could be a sign of dental trouble, such as uneven or sharp teeth.

farrier—a person who takes care of a horse's hooves
vaccination—a shot of medicine that protects from a disease
obesity—to be extremely overweight

NUZZLE UP

When you first bring your miniature horse home, give it time to adjust to its new surroundings. Gaining the trust of a miniature horse takes time. Get to know each other slowly. Spend time talking to your horse in a calm voice. Give it small treats. Pet and brush your horse so it gets used to your touch. Horses have a blind spot and cannot see directly behind themselves. Do not to stand directly behind your horse or touch it from behind. It may kick its legs at you.

Soon your miniature horse will become comfortable having you near. It may even try to **nuzzle** up to you. Other members of your family should also spend time with the miniature horse. If you have other pets at home, introduce them to your miniature horse slowly so they become comfortable with each other.

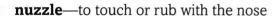

nuzzle—to touch or rub with the nose

Miniature horses can get along with other pets at home.

Miniature horse owners enjoy teaching their pets to do fun tricks.

DID YOU KNOW?

A miniature horse from Australia holds the Guinness World Record for the highest jump. The horse, named Castrawes Paleface Orion, jumped 3 feet, 6.5 inches (1.1 meters).

TEACH YOUR HORSE NEW TRICKS

Miniature horses are very smart. You can train them to do tricks, but it takes time and patience. Before you begin, speak with a horse trainer about how best to train your horse. Have a parent help you research information online about horse training.

Start out with easy tasks, such as how to turn and stop on command. Then build up to more complicated activities, such as how to pull a cart or jump. Be consistent and repetitive with your horse. Repeat an activity until your horse has mastered it. Give it positive feedback, such as petting its neck and using encouraging words. Some owners also use small treats.

If you want your miniature horse to compete in shows, you will need to spend even more time with it. Show horses must learn complicated moves and jumps. You may want to hire a professional miniature horse trainer. This person can help you train your horse to get it ready for shows.

HORSING AROUND

The key to a happy miniature horse is to keep it healthy. Make sure you give it lots of room to run and play. Spend time with your miniature horse. Run alongside it or throw a ball for it to chase. Keeping your horse active also helps to prevent weight gain. Miniature horses like to be with other animals. Consider getting a companion animal if you have the room and time to care for it. Another miniature horse or a goat, sheep, or pig would make a great buddy for this pet.

Be sure your horse does not get bored. This is especially important if it spends many hours alone in its stable. Find activities to keep your horse busy. Miniature horses love to play with large exercise balls. Some owners make a food ball for their pet. Buy a plastic ball with holes from a pet store and put snacks inside. Your horse will spend lots of time trying to get the food out of the ball. Another way to keep your pet active and interested is to create an obstacle course in your yard. You may be surprised at how fast your horse can learn the course.

Make sure your miniature horse has plenty of room to explore.

CHAPTER 4
PART OF THE COMMUNITY

Miniature horses are comfortable around people. They can even lend a helping hand—or hoof. Some miniature horses act as therapy pets. Therapy pets provide comfort, enjoyment, and help for people with disabilities. Because of their gentle nature, miniature horses make great therapy pets. These miniature horses visit nursing homes and hospitals. They help ease anxiety and comfort people who do not feel well. Other miniature horses visit schools and libraries. There, horse owners educate people about the animal.

NERVOUS FLYER? PET A MINIATURE HORSE

Airplane travel can be stressful. Some airports bring in trained animals to cheer up travelers and calm their nerves. Miniature horses visit the Cincinnati/Northern Kentucky International Airport twice a month. People pet and talk to the horses.

A seeing eye horse works similarly to a seeing eye dog. The mini horse guides its owner around the community so that those who cannot see have more independence.

Miniature horses are smart, focused, and have strong vision. This makes them good guides for the visually impaired. These miniature horses are trained to guide their owners wherever they need to go. They may go to the supermarket, walk along city streets, or visit friends. Miniature horses can live to be 20 to 30 years old. Their long lives allow for strong bonds with their owners, making them great guide pets.

BUDDIES FOR LIFE

Every miniature horse has a unique personality. Whether it's just for companionship or for competing in horse shows, your miniature horse will form a lifelong bond with you. Miniature horses can become part of the family for many years.

THE TINIEST MINIS

The Guinness World Record for the world's smallest living male horse goes to Charly, an Arabian horse in Italy. Charly is just 25 inches (63.5 cm) tall. The smallest female horse is named Thumbelina. She tops out at 17.5 inches (44.5 cm) tall.

Thumbelina meets a big horse.

A miniature horse and its owner can share many fun years together.

Miniature horses are a lot of work, but they can be very rewarding. Take time to learn all about them. Read more books about them. Have a parent help you research more about miniature horses online. Consider joining a miniature horse club. Get to know other horse owners. Maybe there is a miniature horse show in your area that you can attend. The more you know about these amazing animals, the better you can care for one.

GLOSSARY

acre (AY-kur)—a measurement of area equal to 43,560 square feet (4,047 square meters); an acre is about the size of a football field

affectionate (uh-FEK-shuh-nit)—showing a great liking for someone or something

ancestor (AN-sess-tur)—a distant relative from long ago

breeder (BREE-der)—a person who raises animals to sell

descendant (dih-SEN-dent)—a person or animal who comes from a common group of people or animals from the past

domesticate (duh-MESS-tuh-kate)—to tame something so that it can live with or be used by humans

digestive system (dye-JESS-tiv SISS-tuhm)—the body organs that break down food into energy and get rid of waste

farrier (FAE-ri-er)—a person who takes care of a horse's hooves

geld (GELD)—to operate on a male animal so it is unable to produce young

graze (GRAYZ)—to eat grass that is growing in a field

nuzzle (NUHZ-uhl)—to touch or rub with the nose

obesity (oh-BEE-sih-tee)—to be extremely overweight

vaccination (vak-sih-NAY-shun)—a shot of medicine that protects from a disease

whinny (WIN-ee)—a gentle, high-pitched sound; the word is often used to describe horse sounds

READ MORE

Bratton, Donna Bowman. *From Head to Tail: All about Horse Care.* Crazy about Horses. North Mankato, Minn.: Capstone Press, 2014.

Gale, Kendra. *The Big Book of Miniature Horses: Everything You Need to Know to Buy, Care for, Train, Show, Breed, and Enjoy a Miniature Horse.* North Pomfret, Vt.: Trafalgar Square Books, 2017.

Matzke, Anne. *Mini Horse.* You Have a Pet What?! Vero Beach, Fla.: Rosen Educational Media, 2015.

Thatcher, Henry. *Clydesdales and Miniature Horses.* Big Animals, Small Animals. New York: PowerKids Press, 2014.

Wood, Alix. *Miniature Horses.* Mini Animals. New York: Rosen Publishing, 2017.

INTERNET SITES

Use FactHound to find Internet sites related to this book.

Visit *www.facthound.com*

Just type in 9781543530599 and go.

 Check out projects, games and lots more at **www.capstonekids.com**

INDEX